Native Americans

Chickasaw

Barbara A. Gray-Kanatiiosh

ABDO Publishing Company

visit us at
www.abdopublishing.com

Cover Photo: Marilyn "Angel" Wynn/Nativestock.com
Interior Photos: Chickasaw Nation p. 30; Corbis pp. 4, 29; Nativestock.com p. 29
Illustrations: David Kanietakeron Fadden pp. 7, 9, 11, 13, 15, 17, 19, 21, 23, 25, 27
Editors: Rochelle Baltzer, Megan M. Gunderson
Art Direction & Maps: Neil Klinepier
Special thanks to the Chickasaw Nation for its contribution and assistance.

Library of Congress Cataloging-in-Publication Data
Gray-Kanatiiosh, Barbara A., 1963-
  Chickasaw / Barbara A. Gray-Kanatiiosh.
    p. cm. -- (Native Americans)
  Summary: An introduction to the history and past and present social life and culture of the Chickasaw Indians, whose homeland was in the southeastern United States.
  Includes bibliographical references and index.
  ISBN-10 1-59197-652-9
  ISBN-13 978-1-59197-652-3
  1. Chickasaw Indians--History--Juvenile literature. 2. Chickasaw Indians--Social life and customs--Juvenile literature. [1. Chickasaw Indians. 2. Indians of North America.] I. Title. II. Series: Native Americans (Edina, Minn.)

E99.C55G73 2006
976.004'97386--dc22   2003069306

About the Author: Barbara A. Gray-Kanatiiosh, JD
Barbara Gray-Kanatiiosh, JD, Ph.D. ABD, is an Akwesasne Mohawk. She resides at the Mohawk Nation and is of the Wolf Clan. She has a Juris Doctorate from Arizona State University, where she was one of the first recipients of ASU's special certificate in Indian Law. Barbara's Ph.D. is in Justice Studies at ASU. She is currently working on her dissertation, which concerns the impacts of environmental injustice on indigenous culture. Barbara works hard to educate children about Native Americans through her writing and Web site, where children may ask questions and receive a written response about the Haudenosaunee culture. The Web site is: www.peace4turtleisland.org

About the Illustrator: David Kanietakeron Fadden
David Kanietakeron Fadden is a member of the Akwesasne Mohawk Wolf Clan. His work has appeared in publications such as *Akwesasne Notes*, *Indian Time*, and the *Northeast Indian Quarterly*. Examples of his work have also appeared in various publications of the Six Nations Indian Museum in Onchiota, NY. His work has also appeared in "How the West Was Lost: Always the Enemy," produced by Gannett Production, which appeared on the Discovery Channel. David's work has been exhibited in Albany, NY; the Lake Placid Center for the Arts; Centre Strathearn in Montreal, Quebec; North Country Community College in Saranac Lake, NY; Paul Smith's College in Paul Smiths, NY; and at the Unison Arts & Learning Center in New Paltz, NY.

Contents

Where They Lived

The Chickasaw (CHIH-kuh-saw) spoke a **dialect** of the Muskogean language family. Many tribes along the lower Mississippi River valley spoke this dialect. The Chickasaw language and **culture** were similar to those of their neighbor, the Choctaw. Other nearby tribes included the Quapaw, Cherokee, Creek, and Tunica.

The Chickasaw homelands were located in the Southeast. Chickasaw territory covered northern Mississippi and Alabama, as well as parts of Tennessee and Kentucky. The Mississippi River formed the area's western boundary.

Many different features were found on Chickasaw land. There were rolling hills, vast grasslands, thick forests, and swamps. Oak and hickory trees filled the forests, and

Rock Creek is in the Chickasaw National Recreation Area in Oklahoma. Chickasaw homelands had many creeks and streams, too.

bald cypress trees grew in the swamps.

Various types of animals made their homes near the rivers, streams, and swamps. These animals included ducks, geese, warblers, salamanders, frogs, and snakes. Some snakes were poisonous, such as water moccasins, copperheads, and rattlesnakes.

Chickasaw Homelands

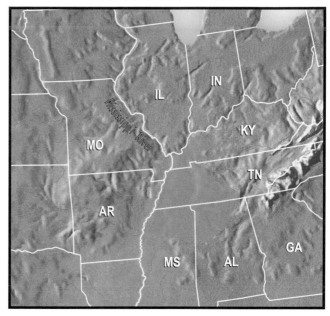

Society

Chickasaw villages were built far apart from each other. This prevented illnesses from spreading throughout the entire Chickasaw community. Typically, the villages were 10 to 15 miles (16 to 24 km) long and up to 4 miles (6 km) wide. The Chickasaw built their villages near waterways. That way, food and water were easily available.

Chickasaw society was matrilineal, so **clan** names were passed on from mother to child. Animals were sacred to the Chickasaw. So, clans bore names such as Fish, Bird, Alligator, and Wolf.

A chief called a *minko* and a council of elders governed each Chickasaw clan. Minkos were elected for life by the council of elders. The council chose them for their wisdom, bravery, and love of the people.

The high minko was at the top of Chickasaw society. This was an inherited position. The high minko maintained the well-being of the people. He also oversaw important decisions that the other minkos made.

Minkos were very wise.
Chickasaw people looked
to them for advice.

Food

The Chickasaw hunted, fished, gardened, and gathered. The men hunted buffalo, deer, and bear with bows and arrows. They used traps to catch smaller animals such as rabbits, squirrels, ducks, and geese.

Every autumn, the men went on a hunting trip. They brought home their catches and gave some to the elders. Then, the women prepared the meat for meals and to store for winter. Sometimes, they smoked strips of meat over a fire.

Men fished for catfish, drum, perch, bass, and suckers. They used spears, nets, traps, and hooks and lines to catch them. Sometimes, they put a mixture of crushed green walnut hulls into deep water. This mixture forced fish into more shallow water. Then, the fish were easier to catch.

Both men and women gardened. The men prepared the fields for planting. Then, the women planted and tended the gardens. The Chickasaw grew corn, beans, peas, melons, pumpkins, and sunflowers. Corn was especially important for food and trade.

Women gathered food for their families. They collected wild onions, plums, berries, nuts, and grapes. They used wild roots and herbs to make tea. And to make medicine drinks, they used herbs and sassafras leaves.

Spearfishing was a common way for the Chickasaw to obtain meals.

Homes

Chickasaw families owned both summer and winter homes. Their summer homes were rectangular. These homes had sloped, triangular roofs. Chickasaw winter homes were circular and were built using **wattle and daub**.

Summer homes were about 12 feet (4 m) wide and 22 feet (7 m) long. The Chickasaw used wooden poles to construct a frame. Then, they covered the frame with mats of bark or grass. They left small openings in the walls for air to pass through.

Chickasaw winter homes were about 25 feet (8 m) in **diameter**. The Chickasaw used pine logs to form a frame over a shallow pit. This helped to warm the home. They covered the frame with woven mats of reeds or grass. Finally, they coated the outside and inside with mud. This also warmed the home. And, it protected the interior from wind, rain, and snow.

Both summer and winter homes had a door opening on one side. The Chickasaw covered this opening with a woven mat or an animal hide. They used branches to make their beds and animal hides or furs to cover them.

The summer home *(left)* was divided down the center into two rooms. Years later, pioneers used this design for log cabins.

The winter home *(right)* was designed to protect the Chickasaw from harsh weather.

Clothing

The Chickasaw wore clothing made from animal hides and plant materials. The women wore dresses, and the men wore **breechcloths** and shirts. To protect their feet, both men and women wore moccasins.

The women made the clothing. To make a piece of clothing from an animal hide, they first scraped away the extra meat. Then, they **tanned** the hide. This process made the material soft enough to work with. The women used **awls** and needles made of bone to help them sew. And, they used thread made of deer **sinew** or plant fibers.

In cold weather, the Chickasaw wore robes made of buffalo or bear furs. And, the men wore tall deerskin boots. These boots kept them warm and protected their legs from brush and thorns.

The women wore mantles around their shoulders. These mantles were made from plant fibers and animal hides. Some men wore mantles made of swan feathers. These were prized. This type of mantle was the most honorable badge that a Chickasaw warrior could gain.

Both men and women wore their hair long. Men used clamshells to pluck their facial and body hair. Sometimes, the Chickasaw **tattooed** their bodies. During ceremonies or wars, warriors wore face paint made from minerals or plants. Individuals were recognized by their own painted design.

The Chickasaw wore mantles around their shoulders. Men's swan-feather mantles were very special.

13

Crafts

Every tool that the Chickasaw used was built from natural materials. Cane was an especially useful plant for the tribe. The Chickasaw used strips of cane to weave baskets and mats. And, they used pieces of hollowed cane to construct blowguns. The tribe also made cane fish traps.

Pottery was another important craft for the Chickasaw. They used clay pots to hold water and to cook and store food. To make a pot, Chickasaw women first gathered clay from riverbanks. Then, they rolled the clay and shaped it to form a pot. Next, they placed the pot in a pit to cook. Finally, they decorated the top of the pot with line designs.

Dugout canoes were a common mode of transportation for the Chickasaw. The tribe used them to hunt, fish, visit friends, and deliver trade goods. They made these canoes from trees with straight, wide trunks. Men used fire and stone axes to cut down the trees. Then, they removed the bark and carved the canoes.

Chickasaw men used fire, stone tools, and clamshells to carve canoes.

Family

The Chickasaw married between **clans**. When a man wished to marry, he gave the woman's sister or mother a fine gift. If the woman's parents approved, she received the gift. Then she told her family her answer, while the man waited for the news.

Chickasaw villages contained **extended families**. Each family member was expected to contribute to the survival of the village. Both men and women were in charge of certain tasks.

Families often attended ceremonies together. There, they sang, feasted, and danced. At some ceremonies they played games. Both men and women played *akabatle*. In this game, teams hit a figure on top of a pole to score a point. The team that hit the figure the most won. The Chickasaw continue to play this game today.

Men played *toli* and *chunkey*. *Toli* players used two netted rackets to launch a deerskin ball into the opponent's goal. To begin the game of *chunkey*, someone rolled a stone. Then, players threw spears to where they thought the stone would stop. The man who threw his spear closest to where the stone landed was the winner.

Chickasaw men enjoyed playing *toli*. This game is similar to present-day lacrosse.

Children

Chickasaw adults were responsible for raising the children in their **clan**. Elders taught children about the tribe's history and **culture**. And, girls and boys learned many things by helping with daily tasks. They helped weed and plant gardens. They also gathered nuts and berries. Although the children often helped the adults, they still had plenty of time to play.

Women taught girls how to identify plants, prepare food, and make clothing. The girls learned to grind corn with a **pestle** and **mortar**. They also learned how to make sewing needles from fish bones. And, the girls were taught how to melt bear fat. The tribe used this fat as cooking oil and as hair and body lotion.

Boys learned how to hunt and build hunting tools. Young men ages 12 to 15 were assigned to elders to learn hunting skills. As part of their training, the boys used blowguns to hunt small animals. Blowguns used wooden darts with dandelion down attached to one end. When air was blown into the gun, the dart shot out of the opposite end.

Chickasaw men taught the
boys how to use blowguns.

19

Myths

Native Americans pass on myths, or stories, through many generations. The following is a Chickasaw **migration** myth. It explains how the tribe found their homelands.

Long ago, the Chickasaw lived in western North America. They were unhappy there. So, they asked the Great Spirit for help. He gave them a long pole and a great white dog. The Great Spirit said, "The pole will guide you to a better place, and the dog will protect you."

That evening, the group placed the pole straight up in the ground. The next morning, the pole leaned eastward. So, the tribe began migrating in that direction.

During the trip, poisonous snakes bit some of the people. Fortunately, the dog had special healing powers. When it licked the wounds, the people were healed.

Every night, the pole was placed in the ground. And each morning, the group traveled in the direction that it leaned. Eventually, the tribe crossed the Mississippi River.

The next morning, the pole swayed. Part of the group took this a sign that they were to remain there. This group became known as the Choctaw. The other part of the group continued on and became the Chickasaw.

According to Chickasaw myth, the pole and the great white dog led the Chickasaw to their homelands.

21

War

The Chickasaw sometimes had to fight to protect their land and families. Before a war began, several **rituals** took place to prepare Chickasaw warriors for battle. The warriors **fasted** for three days and nights. Then, a war dance was held. After the dance, tribal chiefs told stories of brave Chickasaw fighters to encourage the warriors.

During battle, Chickasaw warriors used spears and bows and arrows. For close combat, they used knives and **hatchets** made of stone or antlers. They also used war clubs made of stone or carved tree roots.

Chickasaw weaponry changed when they began trading with the Europeans. The tribe started to use guns, metal arrowheads, and metal knives during battle.

The Chickasaw celebrated their war victories. Villages gathered to sing and dance. And, everyone listened to the warriors share their stories.

Neighboring tribes knew the Chickasaw as fierce warriors.

23

Contact with Europeans

The Chickasaw first met Europeans in 1540. That December, Spaniard Hernando de Soto's expedition reached the Tombigbee River in present-day Mississippi. Chickasaw territory was on the opposite side of the river. Tribal warriors warned the Spaniards not to enter their land. However, the Spaniards eventually crossed the river into Chickasaw territory.

Then, de Soto's group captured several Chickasaw men and demanded to see their chiefs. The chiefs arrived with gifts of animal skins, shawls, and furs. But de Soto was not as friendly. He forced the chiefs to provide his group with food and shelter for the winter.

In early March, the Spaniards were ready to move on. De Soto demanded that 200 Chickasaw warriors carry his group's supplies. The Chickasaw felt insulted, so several warriors set fire to the Spanish camp. Soon after, the Spaniards left the area.

Europeans did not return to Chickasaw land until almost 150 years later. Jacques Marquette and Louis Jolliet arrived in 1673. They were the first French explorers in the area.

Then in 1698, British traders Thomas Welch and Anthony Dodsworth arrived. The Chickasaw liked trading with the British because they had superior goods. The Chickasaw received cotton cloth from them, as well as metal tools and weapons. Eventually, the Chickasaw and the British formed an **alliance**.

Jacques Marquette and Louis Jolliet were the first French explorers to enter Chickasaw territory.

Tishomingo

Tishomingo was a skilled Chickasaw warrior and chief. He proudly fought to protect his people and their land. He was respected and loved among the Chickasaw. His name means "medicine chief."

When the United States warred against hostile northwestern tribes, Tishomingo came to its aid. He served with General Anthony Wayne. For his service, President George Washington awarded Tishomingo a silver medal. Tishomingo cherished this medal for the rest of his life.

Between 1837 and 1838, Tishomingo and his people were removed from their homelands. During their journey, Tishomingo died. He was 102 years old.

Tishomingo was the last Chickasaw war chief before the tribe was relocated. In 1856, the capital of the Chickasaw Nation was named Tishomingo City to honor the beloved chief.

Tishomingo was respected among the Chickasaw. Today, he is fondly remembered.

The Chickasaw Today

In 1830, the United States passed the Indian Removal Act. The purpose of this act was to free up more land for new settlers. So, the federal government relocated the Native Americans to land west of the Mississippi River. Many northern tribes settled in the new territory.

The federal government had more difficulties moving the southeastern tribes. The Five Civilized Tribes resisted. This group consisted of the Chickasaw, Cherokee, Choctaw, Seminole, and Creek. These tribes refused to trade their rich lands for unfamiliar territory.

Still, the U.S. military forced the Five Civilized Tribes westward to present-day Oklahoma. Many of them died while on the journey or soon afterward. They suffered from diseases such as smallpox, cholera, food poisoning, and malnourishment.

In 2000, there were 38,351 Chickasaw. Today, the Chickasaw Nation is located in south-central Oklahoma. It is a **federally recognized** tribe. The Chickasaw Nation operates several educational programs. These include early childhood education, higher education, and job training. The Chickasaw Nation also aims to preserve tribal language and traditions. Classes are offered in Chickasaw history, dancing, and crafts.

The Chickasaw continue to hold tribal celebrations. Chickasaw Brad Smith wears Fancy Dance clothing of the pow-wow style for a tribal festival.

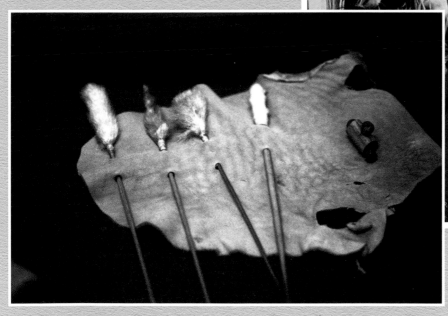

At one time, the Chickasaw used blowguns to hunt. Today, traditional blowgun darts are displayed at museums or cultural centers.

The official flag of the Chickasaw Nation

Governor of the Chickasaw Nation Bill Anoatubby (left), and Seminole artist Enoch Kelly Haney (right) stand in front of the Chickasaw Warrior sculpture that Haney created. The statue was unveiled on May 10, 2005.

The 2005-2006 annual Chickasaw Princess Pageant winners were (left to right) Chickasaw Junior Princess Jaisen Monetathchi, Little Miss Chickasaw Halley Taylor, and Chickasaw Princess Tamela Alexander.

Glossary

alliance - people, groups, or nations joined for a common cause.

awl - a pointed tool for making small holes in materials such as leather or wood.

breechcloth - a piece of hide or cloth, usually worn by men, that wraps between the legs and ties with a belt around the waist.

clan - an extended family related by a shared symbol.

culture - the customs, arts, and tools of a nation or people at a certain time.

dialect - a form of a language spoken in a certain area or by certain people.

diameter - the distance across the middle of a circle.

extended family - a family that includes grandparents, uncles, aunts, and cousins in addition to a mother, father, and children.

fast - to go without food.

federal recognition - the U.S. government's recognition of a tribe as being an independent nation. The tribe is then eligible for special funding and for protection of its reservation lands.

hatchet - a short-handled ax often with a hammerhead to be used with one hand.

migrate - to move from one place to another, often to find food.

mortar - a strong bowl or cup in which a material is pounded.

pestle - a club-shaped tool used to pound or crush a substance.

ritual - a form or order to a ceremony.

sinew - a band of tough fibers that joins a muscle to a bone.

tan - to make a hide into leather by soaking it in a special liquid.

tattoo - a permanent design made on the skin.

wattle and daub - a construction method. Wattle consists of a framework of sticks and twigs. It is covered with daub, a mixture of sand and clay.

Web Sites

To learn more about the Chickasaw, visit ABDO Publishing Company on the World Wide Web at **www.abdopublishing.com**. Web sites about the Chickasaw are featured on our Book Links page. These links are routinely monitored and updated to provide the most current information available.

Index